What sort of a man was Bismarck? Was he really the emotional child who burst into tears when he couldn't get his own way with the Kaiser? Or were his rages carefully calculated, just like his secret rewriting of an official telegram to provoke France into war? Was the statesman who created a united Germany from thirty-nine squabbling states a temperamental neurotic, a master diplomat—or was he both?

In 1848 Germany had no capital city, no national identity and little influence on the outside world. By the time Bismarck left office as Chancellor in 1890, the German Empire was perhaps the greatest power in Europe. "The great questions of the day will not be decided by speeches ... but by iron and blood," announced Bismarck in 1863. This attitude led to short and successful wars with Austria in 1866 and France in 1870. But, as Richard Kisch explains, Bismarck wanted peace and security for Germany, rather than military glory. To this end, he devised an ingenious system of foreign alliances, and introduced enlightened social reforms.

This vividly illustrated book analyses the character and politics of a fascinating man. When Bismarck was rejected by an ungrateful Kaiser, his intricate system for preserving peace collapsed, and twenty years later Europe was thrown into the First World War.

The "Iron Chancellor", Prince
Leopold Otto von Bismarck.

Bismarck

Richard Kisch

WAYLAND PUBLISHERS

More Wayland History Makers

SBN 85340 303 1

Copyright © 1976 by Wayland (Publishers) Ltd
49 Lansdowne Place Hove East Sussex BN3 1HS
Text set in 12/13 pt. Photon Baskerville, printed by photolithography,
and bound in Great Britain at The Pitman Press, Bath

Contents

List of Illustrations

1 Introduction

Prince Otto Leopold von Bismarck was the dominant political personality in Europe in the second half of the nineteenth century. He was regarded, universally, as the "Iron Chancellor". He brought together and created the state of Germany under Prussian leadership. He transformed a jigsaw puzzle of some thirty-nine independent territories with their own rulers, courts, armies and religious, cultural and linguistic traditions into one unified state. The new empire included the kingdoms of Bavaria, Saxony, Wurtemburg, Hanover (which had a dynastic link with England) and the duchy of Schleswig-Holstein. Under Bismarck, for the first time in history, the Germanic peoples acquired a single national identity, as well as a capital city (Berlin) and a constitution.

Bismarck came to power in Prussia in 1862, and he did so by saving the monarchy from a constitutional crisis. He insisted that King William I should tear up a signed abdication statement. He agreed to take over only if he was given a completely free hand. He became Minister-President; his power was virtually dictatorial. He would have nothing to do with any form of parliamentary control over the executive; nor with the Liberals, who wanted a limited democracy and "constitutional rights" to protect themselves from tyrannical rule by the monarchy. He had a deep-rooted hatred of parliamentary institutions on the British model. This was to influence him as much as his attitude to France.

> "It is not by speeches and majority resolutions that the great questions of the day are settled. That was the mistake of 1848 and 1849. It is by iron and blood." *Otto von Bismarck*

Opposite Otto von Bismarck pictured next to his wife, Johanna von Puttkamer, just after their wedding and just before Bismarck's rise to power.

> "I have great respect for my dog's knowledge of human character. He is quicker and more thorough than I."
> *Otto von Bismarck*

Below William I, Emperor of Germany and King of Prussia, who was completely dominated by Bismarck.

For Bismarck France was the implacable enemy. He was determined to stop any chance of another Napoleon, let alone a further French revolutionary challenge to Europe. He was just as determined to establish a sovereign German state separate from the Austrian Empire and the domineering control of the Hapsburg dynasty.

Bismarck never made any secret of all this. In fact, he made a point of declaring his intentions in advance. It confused his opponents. They did not know whether to believe him or not. When he warned the French Emperor Napoleon III of his plan to unify Germany under Prussian leadership it was dismissed as "bluff!" But Benjamin Disraeli in Britain was shrewder; the future Lord Beaconsfield tapped his nose when he heard what Bismarck had to say. "Beware of that man," he told his friends, "he means what he says."

When industrialization brought wealth to Germany, the army was reorganized under the Iron Chancellor. Its mobility and supply services were transformed; so was its firepower, the product of a fast-growing German armaments industry. The railways were nationalized, which meant that conscripts could be mobilized much faster; this played a big part in causing the devastating defeat of France in the 1870 Franco-Prussian war.

For twenty years after King William I of Prussia was proclaimed Kaiser (Emperor of Germany) in the Hall of Mirrors at Versailles, Bismarck's foreign policy (the so-called *pax Germanicus*) guaranteed European peace and stability. But even then the seeds of far more violent and bloody conflicts were germinating as Germany joined Britain, France, the United States, Russia and others in a fast and furious colonial carve-up of Africa, Latin America and the Far East.

In Germany itself, Bismarck dominated domestic politics through the sheer force of his personality and the shrewdness of his parliamentary tactics. Contemptuous of the opposition parties in the Reichstag (the Federal parliament), he was always capable of outflanking them. He would completely change his policies

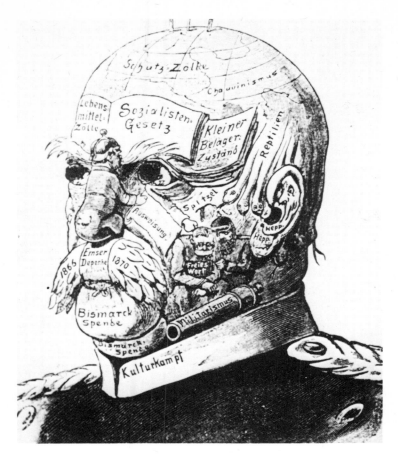

Labels in the caricature:
Schutz Zolle · Chauvinismus · Lebens mittel-Zölle · Sozialisten-Gesetz · Kleiner Belager-Zustand · Reptilien · Spitzel · Ausweisung · Hepp · Emser Depeche · 1866 · 1870 · Frei's Wort · Bismarck Spende · Militarismus · Kulturkampf

Left One view of Bismarck's career: a caricature of Bismarck's "achievements". They include martial law, bribed journalism, aggression, faked diplomatic documents, suppression of religion and bans on free speech.

whenever it suited his purpose. Nobody could anticipate his next move, let alone understand his motives. "He tried posing as a liberal but nobody could take him seriously as a radical," said the English historian, A.J.P. Taylor.

Yet Bismarck was not altogether as autocratic and dictatorial as is sometimes stated. His social policy, which was run on the same practical lines as his foreign policy, was both far-sighted and compassionate. Frank Harris, the Victorian writer and gossip, knew Bismarck as a fellow student at Gottingen University; he wrote: "If he had not been a junker in a privileged position, he might have been as great a social reformer as any."

RUINS OF EMPIRE.

SHADE OF BISMARCK. "I BUILT WITH BLOOD AND IRON, AND ONLY BLOOD REMAINS."

As it was, Bismarck proved a past master at stealing ideas from the liberals and making it seem they had come from the conservatives. The world's first industrial insurance scheme for workers was introduced in Germany while he was Chancellor. So were state pensions, and industrial accident and health laws. Universal adult suffrage for men was introduced in Germany at a time when most Englishmen had no vote at all.

The extraordinary achievement of this exceptionally talented, shrewd, farseeing, sometimes charming, autocratic Prussian junker (derivation: *junc,* young + *herr,* sir) contrasts with his calculated, cunning, capricious, cynical and sometimes contemptible methods.

Otto von Bismarck bestrode the peace of Europe like a colossus in the later nineteenth century. But sadly, his policy set the stage for future wars and tragedies to come. He knew only too well what could happen under his successors. In one fearful moment he even foresaw the twilight of the Gods and the total collapse of the system he did so much to create.

The date he put on it was November, 1918.

Opposite Punch's illustration of the collapse of the balance of power in Europe, which Bismarck had created single-handed. At the end of his life, Bismarck himself predicted that his *Pax Germanicus* would only last until 1918.

2 Mad Junker

Otto Eduard Leopold von Bismarck was born on 1st April, 1815, at Schoenhausen, the family estate about sixty miles from Berlin. His father, Ferdinand, was a typical ponderous Prussian squire. Like most Pomeranian junkers he lived by working his land rather than, as in England, living off rents. Otto's mother, Wilhelmine, was quite the opposite of her husband. She was a frustrated intellectual who did not like the country. A very strong, ambitious woman, she was determined that her children should have an intellectual education, and drove them on without giving them much love. Otto hated her and revered his father. But, although he inherited his father's strong physique and appetites, his mind and temperament were like his mother's. Otto grew to be a huge man who ate and drank too much and walked stiffly like an officer. Yet he had delicate, artistic hands, a small head and sensitive mouth. He also had a surprisingly squeaky voice.

The Bismarcks had always been attached to the Prussian court. They had served the ruling Hohenzollern dynasty, as chamberlains and officials with unswerving loyalty—if not with distinction—for as long as anyone could remember. Young Otto was always part of the royal circle. He was treated as one of the family, and spent much of his time with the younger Hohenzollerns.

Bismarck's schooling was chosen for him by his mother, who sent him to the Planum Academy in Berlin. This school had a reputation for rigorous discipline and

Below Bismarck's father, Karl Wilhelm Ferdinand, whom Bismarck admired and respected.

a spartan way of life. Bismarck later used to say that his mother had packed him off to the most brutal Prussian school "to break my autocratic spirit." He was not an academic success; his early reports reflect the dissatisfaction of his teachers. He was one of those boys, not unlike the future Winston Churchill, who never seemed to fulfil his teachers' hopes. People always thought he could do better.

However, there was a hint of progress when he went to study at the Kloster Gymnasium in 1828. Professor Bonnel, his tutor, summed up the general view of the 13-year-old Bismarck: "Otto is a bright boy."

This view may not have been shared so readily by the Rector of Gottingen University in Hanover. Bismarck arrived there in 1832 to study law. As an undergraduate, he quickly gained a reputation as a young buck. He had a gargantuan appetite, an unslakeable thirst, a love of garish, eccentric clothing. He was a gay carefree student indulging in the excitement of romantic adventures and affairs of the heart. He acquired a reputation as the "Mad Junker." He also had an acid tongue and sharp wit. He was invariably accompanied by a large mastiff hound. More significantly, perhaps, he discovered a talent for debate and a gift of repartee.

Politically, Bismarck found himself swept along in the wave of reforming zeal and liberalism that followed the post-war congress in Vienna (1815). A feeling of social change and constitutional reform was very much in the air in the Universities—especially at Gottingen. At first, Bismarck posed as a radical at university and at court, but found himself befriended by bourgeois intellectuals whom he despised both as a class and as individuals. He therefore stopped going to political meetings of the revolutionary *Burschenshaften,* the students' unions; instead he joined an aristocratic student-corps, the elite Hanover Corps. There was a great deal of swaggering, duelling and boasting; sword cuts were given and taken. Bismarck always maintained a sabre-rattling pose but he was adroit at sidestepping head-on a confrontation, unless it was he who set it up. The only time he received a

Above **Bismarck's mother, Louise Wilhelmine, whom he hated for her lack of love towards him.**

"I am full of prejudices sucked in with Mother's milk." *Otto von Bismarck*

15

Above An idealized drawing of the youthful Bismarck, who had a huge physique, squeaky voice and an explosive temper.

minor duelling injury he characteristically dismissed it as a foul.

The Rector of Gottingen also had a foretaste of Bismarckian tactics, of the future Chancellor's sense of occasion and *realpolitik*. His apparent "bluff" and belligerence was invariably backed up by superb displays of self confidence. Frequently this guaranteed success, if only temporarily, as he discovered when he was disturbed one morning while lounging half-dressed in his room after a riotous night out: the University Proctor arrived to deliver a summons.

It seemed that, the previous night, a window had been broken at the Golden Cross tavern in the town.

"Bismarckus per domine citatus est" (Bismarck is summoned by the Rector) read the Latin script presented by the Proctor.

Incensed by the delivery of such a formal note, the big student flung a large velvet gown over his shoulders, and strode across to the Rector's office. In one hand he dangled the official citation; the other restrained his mastiff on a leash.

The Rector was curt. He affected to ignore the bravado of the student's entrance. "What do you want?"

"Nothing! You, apparently, have something to say to me." The intruder dropped the offending summons onto the Rector's desk.

"In that case," said the Rector quietly, "you will first pay a fine of five talers for the dog. Secondly, be good enough to explain how the window of the Golden Cross tavern came to be broken."

"Presumably a bottle flew out of the window of the Golden Cross of its own volition!"

"Indeed. Would you care to be more explicit?"

The young Bismarck silently leaned forward. He picked up a heavy paperweight lying on the Rector's desk, weighed it casually in the palm of his hand. Then, suddenly, he raised his arm and made as if to throw it through the window.

"Get the idea?" The young man turned and swept out without further comment.

Shortly after this incident, Bismarck left Gottingen. He was there less than a year. He switched universities. He went back to court and spent the next year at the Berlin university. Bismarck used to claim that his debts were responsible for the speed with which he left Gottingen, but the incident with the Rector may have had something to do with it. But his university experiences had an important influence on the young Bismarck. He read widely, his favourite authors being Schiller, Goethe, Byron, Shakespeare and Scott. He also made friends with Alexander Keyserling, a German Baron, and John Motley, an American diplomat and historian—the only lasting friendships of his life.

> "No man should die before having smoked 1,000 cigars and drunk 5,000 bottles of champagne." *Otto von Bismarck*

3 On the Way

In May 1835, after graduating from Berlin University, Bismarck managed to scrape through the entrance examination for the Prussian civil service. Next year, after a few weeks training at Potsdam, he was posted to Aachen, also known as Aix-la-Chapelle, in the Rhineland. He was twenty-one years old.

He did not make a good civil servant. He had no patience for red tape and routine. The civil service was full of busybodies prying into his private affairs. Someone always wanted to know what he was doing, where he had been, why he was late for work.

Nor did the local people of Aachen interest him; they were Roman Catholics with no love of Prussia. They preferred French liberalism and disliked and despised the Prussian administrators. Bismarck reciprocated their dislike.

He showed it, one day, when a riot nearly developed over his unbending Lutheran refusal to bow the neck. It happened when the Junker came across a Catholic street procession, complete with religious banners and relics. Bismarck stubbornly refused to kneel as the Host approached, but stood rigidly upright, without even taking off his hat. A spectator angrily knocked it off and began inciting the crowd against him. An ugly scene began to develop.

Bismarck imperiously slashed his attacker across the face with his cane. Then, without waiting for things to get worse, he dashed into the middle of the road and

Opposite **Bismarck in his youth was an ardent lover and his passion for attractive women continued even when he was in power. Here he is pictured with a well-known singer, Pauline Lucca, in 1865.**

fell in with the military detachment bringing up the rear of the procession. The army, in this case, acted as his shield and armour. Nobody dared to follow, and the provocative Prussian was able to reach his lodging with his escort.

Aachen however had important attractions for Bismarck. In those days it was a key diplomatic and social centre. The international smart set were always coming to it or going from it. The young Junker found plenty of opportunities for widening his social life and diplomatic connections. He was also a compulsive gambler. He cultivated a reputation for chasing women. He was the Great Lover. He seems to have taken a particular fancy for some of the good-looking English girls, who always seemed to be on hand. He became deeply involved with the attractive niece of the Duke of Cleveland, and followed her home to her family estates in the English shires. Then he chased another lass from Leicestershire to London, then to Paris, back across the continent to Aachen, until he finally lost her in Vienna.

During this last affair he overstayed his leave by three months and, rather than return to apologise to his superiors, he began his national service. (Prussians with a university education had to serve twelve months in the army as officers.) Bismarck joined the troops stationed at Potsdam. He hated army life, but managed to exploit his privileged family connections to make things easier. He was always at home at the royal palace and was an intimate friend of the crown prince, the future Frederick William IV.

In 1839, his national service completed, Bismarck resigned from the civil service. He let it be known that: "he by no means intended to be accountable to the government for his personal actions!" He hated established authority, and yet, years later, he would not tolerate disobedience from his subordinates.

Bismarck, now twenty-four, was still unsure of what he wanted to do. At one point he threw in his hand and decided to go home. He spent time as a working land-owner in the true Junker tradition, and joined his elder

"I distrust politicians in long clothes, whether priests or women." *Otto von Bismarck*

brother re-organizing the family estate at Kniephof in Pomerania. He was a regular visitor to cattle markets and horsefairs, later boasting of the experience he acquired when dealing with horse traders. In 1845, when his father died, he took over the other larger family property at Schoenhausen. But during these years Bismarck was far from happy. He was isolated and alone. He was not really interested in farming. He was bored with his neighbours.

In 1844 he decided to give the civil service another try. But this turned out no better than before, and he only lasted two weeks. "I have never been able to put up with superiors," he explained after resigning for the second time.

Above **The Bismarck family residence at Schoenhausen, where Bismarck lived while in the political wilderness in the 1840s.**

Above **Johanna von Puttkamer, Bismarck's deeply religious wife. She helped quell Bismarck's youthful impetuosity, and her Lutheran faith strongly influenced him.**

Fortunately a new lease of life came when he found a wife and a religion. His bride, Johanna von Puttkamer, was a simple, patient woman with a strong Lutheran faith to which Bismarck sincerely subscribed. His new-found religion fitted in with his beliefs about life, teaching that service to the state and to the King was the duty of everyone. More importantly perhaps, Lutheranism helped to calm Bismarck's violent personality and gave him a clear purpose. Armed with religion and a belief in the divine right of princes, Otto von Bismarck could be totally devious and cynical. He believed implicitly in his mission. He was God's witness. "I feel I am serving God when I serve the King," he declared.

At the end of the 1840s, Bismarck was almost ready for the next big move which was to change the pattern of his career. His first taste of public life came about almost by accident when the new King of Prussia, Frederick William IV, summoned a meeting of the so-called United Diet in 1847. This was the nearest thing the Prussians had to a national assembly, and more than Bismarck and his friends wanted.

Bismarck was at the meeting purely by chance; he was only a reserve delegate. But then a regular member retired and Bismarck took his place. He burst on to the floor with an aggressively monarchist speech which produced an uproar, as he complacently noted in his memoirs. He made himself a "King's Champion", attacking every measure the liberals proposed. He did not care whether anyone approved. Indeed, there were signs that the King was embarrassed to have such a violently reactionary supporter. But Bismarck, like other politicians before and since, had sensed the vital need to adopt a style and authority, however provocative, with which to pursue his long term objective—the search for power.

4 Opportunity Knocks

Germany was a slow starter in the international power game, which Bismarck was one day to master. In Europe, during the early 1800s, Belgium and Greece had won their national identity. "Germany" on the other hand was still a loose confederation of Germanic states which had been created at the Congress of Vienna (1815) after the long Napoleonic Wars.

As Professor Medlicott has put it: "Germany had had no religious unity since the sixteenth century. She had no natural centre or capital city. Her frontiers were not defendable and, indeed, in a strategic sense she had no frontiers."

Prussia and Austria were the main elements of the German situation. They had started as partners against Napoleonic France at the beginning of the century, but now they were rivals. Prussia had grown out of the small state of Brandenburg and, even though it had grown very large, was ruled by a small military elite. But its military confidence had been badly shaken in 1806 by the beating handed out by Napoleon at the battle of Jena. Austria, the centre of the great Hapsburg empire, was the acknowledged leader of the confederation. She held the whip hand, and was resented by Prussia.

The smaller German states knew this only too well, and often played Prussia and Austria off against one another. They wanted Austria's protection against Prussia's bullying, but they needed Prussia to protect them from outside threats, especially France, and for

Below Otto von Bismarck in 1848, the year of revolutions in Europe. As he was then a diehard conservative, the liberal resurgence of that year seemed to signal the end of Bismarck's political ambitions.

economic stability. They wanted to keep their independence inside the confederation, rather than to merge into one large state.

But in the 1830s and 1840s there was an agitation for change and for greater national unity. Led by middle-class intellectual liberals the German people slowly came to see themselves as a single nationality. In Prussia, the new King, Frederick William IV, though an autocrat at heart, also aimed at a stronger national unity as a way of challenging Austrian leadership in Germany. Austria in contrast wanted to keep the *status quo*.

The cause of German unity was given even greater impetus by the success of the *Zollverein,* the Customs Union, created in 1834 under Prussian leadership. By abolishing trade duties within its borders and by imposing a uniform tariff on all German territories, a great boost was given to the idea of free trade. By 1844 nearly all Germany was included in this "Common Market." Austria, however, was excluded. In time the small German states became used to Prussia's leadership. The

Below The monument in Berlin to the Prussian soldiers killed while suppressing the liberal revolutions of 1848–49.

Zollverein also gave Prussia even greater economic strength than Austria. Hand in hand with her growing economic power went the need for political change. A new constitution and political and social reforms were now a matter of urgency. The problems thrown up by nationalism and industrialization could only be met by a united Germany.

But the fact remained that forty per cent of the official representation in the Bund, the parliament of the German confederation, were nobles. Their age-old conservatism stood in the way of achieving real national unity. In 1848, however, a great revolutionary surge swept across Europe. France and Italy were engulfed in rebellion. Metternich, the elderly Chancellor of Austria and champion of the old order, fell from power. Street fighting broke out in Berlin and King Frederick William, bowing to the forces of liberalism, agreed to call a Prussian parliament. Bismarck's liberal enemies at the United Diet of 1847 seemed to have won, and there was nothing he could do. Bismarck was not elected either to the German national parliament at Frankfurt or to the Prussian parliament.

Yet neither parliament lasted long. In the autumn Frederick William felt strong enough to disband the radical Prussian parliament and replace it with a much weaker assembly—to which Bismarck was elected. The Frankfurt assembly in its turn broke up at the end of the year once Frederick William had refused their offer of the Imperial Crown and it had become clear that the assembly had no popular support.

To fill the vaccuum left by the collapse of these two assemblies, and as a direct challenge to Austria's leadership of Germany, Frederick William, and his closest adviser Radowice, set up the Erfurt Union. This was in effect a "lesser Germany" made up of most of the northern German states with a parliament and an army controlled by Prussia. Austria was not even consulted about it. Bismarck himself was to create much the same sort of union almost twenty years later. But in 1850 he denounced it: "We are Prussians and want to remain

Above Metternich, the tough conservative Chancellor of Austria who fell from power in 1848 leaving inadequate successors to govern Austria.

"By nature I am Republican but I believe firmly in a future life which is why I am a Royalist." *Otto von Bismarck*

Prussian." It would be better to return to the old order, to " the agreement of Prussia and Austria to control the whole of Germany."

Supported by Russia, Austria took up this Prussian challenge to its authority. Rebellion was stirring in Hesse, one of the small northern German states, and Schwarzenberg, the Austrian Prime Minister, asked the old confederation to let him intervene. By doing so he was effectively threatening Prussian military control of the roads through Hesse. War seemed inevitable. Both sides mobilized, but Prussia shrank from confrontation at the last moment and backed down. At the subsequent settlement at Olomouc, Prussia agreed to dissolve the Erfurt Union and to reconvene the old German confederation under Austrian supremacy. This was one of the biggest humiliations in Prussian history.

Otto von Bismarck, then hibernating in the country surprised his friends by calling for the treaty of Olomouc to be accepted. Since Prussia was weak militarily, he argued that the Erfurt Union would not have helped Prussia to control Germany. But his support for Austria and the Olomouc settlement was a shrewd move. Already Bismarck was looking ahead and planning his future. With the German confederation back in business, Prussia would have to send a delegate to the Diet at Frankfurt. Who better than Bismarck, the one man in Prussia capable of working with Austria? Bismarck himself had no experience of diplomacy but he was not worried. "I shall do my duty. It is God's affair to give me understanding." It was his first high diplomatic post. He was to serve Prussia continuously for the next thirty-nine years.

5 The Rivals

Bismarck went to the Federal Diet ostensibly as a friend of Austria, but he was quick to change his attitude. Austria's success at Olomouc had blinded her to the rising power of Prussia; the arrogance of Austrian diplomats at once antagonized Bismarck. Rather than accept Austrian control of the assembly he became as provocative as possible.

A small incident will serve to show Bismarck's belligerence. On arrival at Frankfurt he was received by the Austrian President of the Diet, Count Thun. The Count was in his shirtsleeves smoking a cigar. Not to be outdone, Bismarck lit his own cigar, so breaking the convention against smoking in the presence of a senior. A running battle now went on in the military committee of the assembly. By tradition, only the Austrian delegates smoked at meetings. Previous Prussian delegates had been high aristocrats and non-smokers. Bismarck had learned to smoke at university. His cigar was a sign that he was a man of a new sort. It was a personal challenge to Austrian supremacy.

Throughout the next few years at Frankfurt, Bismarck committed himself to one policy—conflict with Austria. This was a complete reversal of his stated beliefs. All his reports back to Berlin were based on this one idea. His plan was to bring back Radowice's old idea of a "lesser Germany" made up of the Protestant northern states under Prussian domination. The best way to do this, he felt, was to make some foreign alliances to strengthen Prussia's hand.

"I am no democrat. I was born and raised an aristocrat." *Otto von Bismarck*

Above **Two portraits of Bismarck in the 1850s, when his first battle with Austria, over membership of the** *Zollverein*, **took place.**

Bismarck may have preached conflict with Austria, but Frederick William consistently ignored his advice. In 1854, on the outbreak of the Crimean War, he advised the King to remain isolationist to "frighten Austria." In 1856, he again tried to dictate foreign policy. "Germany is too small for us both," he said of Austria, and repeated that Prussia should look for alliances outside Germany. Once more his advice was ignored.

Yet Bismarck did score one notable victory over Austria in the 1850s despite his relative lack of seniority. Prussia's economy, under the protection of the *Zollverein,* was booming. Austria now asked to be included in it. Bismarck, perhaps without seeing the true consequence of his actions, opposed the idea and managed to put off the decision. Thus, while Prussian coalmines and industry in the Ruhr expanded rapidly,

Austria's economy stagnated. For Prussia, economic independence was soon to mean political and military strength.

Bismarck's hopes for Prussia and his own future were dealt a severe blow in 1858 when King Frederick William went mad. The King's brother William became Regent. William was committed to co-operation with Austria and a more liberal administration at home—the very policies Bismarck totally opposed. Bismarck's future seemed uncertain once again. On the one hand he was unable to work with Austria, and on the other hand he was unwilling to go back to Berlin as a liberal minister. Yet Bismarck was already too important a figure to be ignored. His work at Frankfurt had shown his fighting qualities and, wild reactionary though he seemed to William, he might be useful in the future.

In 1859 he was sent to St. Petersburg in Russia as Prussian Minister. As he himself said, he was "put on ice". Nevertheless, Bismarck enjoyed himself; he liked the Russians and continued to socialize. But his diplomatic comments and advice were either ignored or rejected. In April 1859, Austria went to war in northern Italy against France and Sardinia. It was taken for granted that Prussia would support her. Bismarck took up quite a different line. Take power in northern Germany, he said, and forget the alliance with Austria. But nobody took any notice of him.

Events, however, were soon to turn in Bismarck's favour. In 1860 William I and Albrecht van Roon, his Minister of War, became involved in a constitutional crisis with the Prussian parliament over who should control the army. The struggle dragged on for two years. Nobody would make any concessions.

By September, 1862, King William I was threatening to abdicate. He had reached a deadlock with the parliamentary Chamber. It refused to grant any more money for the army unless he cut the period of military service from three years to two. The King would not give way; his ministers were in despair. There was only one man strong enough to oppose the Chamber and break

Below General Albrecht von Roon, Prussian Minister of War and friend of Bismarck who helped the latter in his rise to power.

Above **The official residence in Berlin, which was only rarely inhabited, of Otto von Bismarck, Prime Minister and Foreign Minister of Prussia.**

the deadlock—Otto von Bismarck. But he refused to do this unless he could have a free hand in foreign policy, and William would not agree to this.

The situation seemed impossible. On 22nd September Bismarck met William at Babelsberg, a summer palace just outside Berlin. The King was armed with a deed of abdication and a programme of foreign policy; if Bismarck argued over the programme, William had decided to produce his written abdication. Bismarck did not even give the King time to go over his programme, "Royal government or the supremacy of parliament" was all that mattered, he said; and he would make sure it was the King who won.

William tore up his act of abdication and his political programme on the spot. Bismarck became Prime

Minister of Prussia. Two weeks later he became Foreign Minister as well. For the next twenty-seven years he was to dominate European politics.

Bismarck recorded his own views of what happened. He wrote in his memoirs: "When I first came into the office, the King showed me his written abdication. I had first of all to re-establish the royal power, for it was shaken and shattered. I was successful. Yet I am not an absolutist. There is always a danger in one-man government. Parliamentary opinion and a free press are necessary to a satisfactory monarchical system."

The reality was that Bismarck, with the help of his friend von Roon, got between the old diehard militarists, the King and parliament. He refused to acknowledge parliament's right to control the army through the military budget. But he also blocked attempts to impose open military dictatorship.

He had arrived at the top.

Left **Bismarck in 1860, Prussian Minister to Russia and on his way up the "greasy pole" of politics.**

6 Prussian Poker

On Schleswig-Holstein: "Only three men have understood the Schleswig-Holstein question. One was Prince Albert. But He is dead. The other was a German Professor who went mad. I am the third—and I've forgotten all about it!" *Lord Palmerston*

Opposite **Benjamin Disraeli**, the future Lord Beaconsfield. "Watch that man," he commented shrewdly after listening to Bismarck, "he means what he says".

The two major powers in Europe, France and Russia, had only vaguely heard of Bismarck before the new Prussian leader began playing international politics seriously. Until then Europe had been dominated by the Franco-Russian alliance. Both Prussia and her more powerful rival, Austria, only affected the balance of power in Europe in a minor way, by acting as buffer states between France and Russia.

At the Prussian helm, Bismarck decisively changed all this. He played diplomacy with the same verve, cynicism and duplicity he used in local politics. His aim was to turn Prussia into a first-rate power and to alter the European balance of power in Prussia's favour.

Benjamin Disraeli, then British Conservative opposition leader, came to know Bismarck when he visited London for the Great Exhibition of 1862. At that time he was Prussian Ambassador to France with a growing reputation for shrewdness. He was received by Lord John Russell, then Prime Minister, and also had a key meeting with the legendary Lord Palmerston.

Disraeli, perhaps, had been specially intrigued to hear that Bismarck had talked to Palmerston about the controversial Danish protectorates over the Duchies of Schleswig and Holstein. Palmerston, it was joked, was one of only three people who had ever understood this obscure problem—and two of them were dead.

After talking to Bismarck at a diplomatic dinner party given by the Russian ambassador in London for the

33

grand Duchess of Saxe-Weimar, Disraeli commented, "Beware of that man, he means what he says."

Disraeli wanted to know, what would Bismarck do if he came to power? Bismarck replied that first he would reorganize the army, with or without the support of parliament; secondly, he would destroy Austrian domination of the German confederation; thirdly, he would unify Germany under Prussian leadership. It was a characteristically straight answer.

Disraeli's opinion of Bismarck was shrewder than that of the French Emperor Napoleon III. Bismarck had outlined a similar plan of action to Napoleon III when they met at Saint Cloud in late September 1862. "The fellow is not serious," commented the French ruler; "he is all bluff!" Within days, Bismarck was Minister-President of Prussia under King William.

Napoleon III was to learn to his cost just how serious Bismarck was. The Prussian had not forgotten that some years earlier Napoleon III had sounded him out about possible Prussian reactions to a French attack on Austria. Bismarck had said: "I am glad for your Majesty's sake that you have imparted this information to the only Prussian diplomat who will not use it to your Majesty's disadvantage. I decline to pass it on because I am convinced, in advance, that my Government will do nothing—and might even prejudice your Majesty's aim." It was clear that Bismarck was plotting Austria's downfall.

Bismarck's first step to realize his plan was taken without support from any political group or party. Within weeks of taking power there was talk of war with Austria. At the Federal Diet Austria was busily trying to strengthen the confederation at Prussia's expense. She demanded membership of the *Zollverein* as Bismarck had promised ten years earlier. Now, however, Bismarck retaliated by signing a commercial treaty with France. It effectively kept Austria out of the *Zollverein* customs union.

At home, he was able to push through plans for massive army reorganization in spite of intense liberal

Opposite **Napoleon III, Emperor of France, who dismissed Bismarck's plans for the unification of Germany as "bluff". Napoleon swiftly learned to his cost just how badly he had misjudged the future "Iron Chancellor".**

opposition. Proposals were passed for changing the basis of compulsory service and speeding up mobilization. Although the liberals in parliament opposed these plans the upper House supported them. Since the constitution called for the agreement of the two Houses, and the King, before money could be spent, there was deadlock. For a time it seemed as if the country was facing yet another crisis. In spite of this Bismarck was able to convince his master that he could keep things under control.

For three years Bismarck used this constitutional deadlock to run Prussia as dictator. He seized every chance to put on warlike demonstrations and to whip up public support with big displays of military strength. He even marched troops into Kassel to frighten the Elector of Hesse, who was defying parliament much as Bismarck himself was defying tradition in Prussia.

Bismarck's big moment came on 30th September, 1862, with a parliamentary speech that put him into the history books as "The Iron Chancellor."

It was an extraordinary occasion, which astonished his friends as much as his enemies. He was obviously nervous and tense. He spoke in short sharp jerks; his voice was even rustier and squeakier than usual. He was intent on forcing through a budget which had earlier been withdrawn although he had tried hard to reduce liberal suspicions of his motives and sincerity.

"The great questions of the day will not be decided by speeches and resolutions of majorities but by iron and blood," he told a surprised Chamber. As always, he did not conceal his meaning. Military strength decided the fate of nations. Though he stressed his desire for settlements he talked chiefly about his aims and ambitions for Prussia. Prussia carried a weight of arms too heavy for her body, he insisted. Now she must use it to the full. Her boundaries were not favourable to a healthy state life.

The speech echoed across Europe. It stimulated and shocked. Both the King and the War Minister, von Roon, were shaken by Bismarck's bluntness.

"I assumed a United Germany was only a matter of time and the North German Confederation was the first step. I did not doubt that a Franco-German war must take place before the construction of a united Germany could be realised. I was preoccupied with the idea of delaying the outbreak of this war until our fighting strength should be increased." *Reflections and Reminiscences. Otto von Bismarck*

The King, indeed, was so depressed by this bombshell that he began talking as though it was all over with the monarchy. He felt he would have to go.

Bismarck shook him out of his gloom and despondency by telling him not to act like Louis XVI of France, but rather as Charles I of England. Even if it means getting badly hurt, one must oppose tyranny, declared Bismarck.

This personal appeal was so successful that the King at once confirmed Bismarck in his job. Until then the appointment had been merely provisional.

The Minister-President of Prussia was now ready for his next move in his plan to destroy Austria.

> "We shall have to fight for our colonies in Europe." *Otto von Bismarck*

Below William I, King of Prussia, enters Berlin for his coronation in 1861. Ten years later he was crowned Emperor of Germany in the "Hall of Mirrors" at Versailles.

7 Blood and Iron

The way was made clear, almost by chance, in 1863 for Bismarck's planned unification of Germany under Prussia. In that year rebellion broke out in Poland, which was then partitioned between Prussia, Austria and Russia. Russia stepped in. Bismarck at first suspected that the Russian Tsar Alexander II wanted to grab Prussian territory in Poland, but he quelled his anxieties and did nothing.

It was a diplomatic master stroke. Greatly to Prussia's benefit the rest of Europe became involved in the Polish affair. A joint Anglo-French press campaign was started. Russia was blamed for what was happening. This destroyed the Franco-Russian alliance and with it the Prussian fear of attack by one or both powers, in the event of a Prussian attack on Austria.

Austria came off badly. The French and English were furious that she had taken no effective supporting action. The Russians were angry that she had even protested. Russo-Austrian relations were strained almost to breaking point. From then on it became increasingly clear that in return for Bismarck's neutrality over Poland, Russia would not take part in any conflict between Austria and Prussia. Bismarck's policy of neutrality had effectively shorn Austria of allies.

Austria's leaders knew quite well that Bismarck was behind it all. Strenuous efforts had been made in diplomatic and court circles to get between Bismarck and his master. But King William was far from being a

Opposite **Franz Josef, Emperor of Austria. His attempts to undermine Bismarck's influence over William I and avoid a confrontation with Prussia failed dismally.**

nonentity. He was shrewd enough to realize that he had a champion of exceptional ability in Otto von Bismarck. Even so, it was hard for him to forget the ties of monarchical sympathy that existed between the German princes.

The Austrian Emperor, Franz Joseph, tried to exploit this personal bond. He proposed a special council of princes to meet at Frankfurt to try yet again to unify Germany peacefully under Austrian leadership.

The invitation to this Council was handed personally to the Prussian King by the King of Saxony. Everything possible was done to persuade King William to accept.

Only Bismarck stood in the way. He was utterly determined that the King should not go. He did not mind how much pressure it took to get his view accepted. It was a psychological struggle of decisive importance between Bismarck and the King. If Bismarck lost, his control of Prussian affairs would also have gone.

Bismarck never left the King's side throughout a series of meetings which continued from spa to spa across Germany. They started at Bad Gastein; then they went to Baden Baden; the end came at Coburg.

The King at last gave in. He was on the verge of hysteria. The invitation was torn up. Bismarck was equally exhausted. He went home in such a state of tension that he burst into tears, smashed a vase and broke the doorhandle of his study. His first major battle with the King had been won. As a result Austria lost the initiative in Germany forever. From then on, Prussia was to assert herself more and more. She would no longer be subservient to Austrian wishes.

The chance for Prussia to show her new-found strength was not long in coming. The catalyst was the Schleswig-Holstein affair (1864). This was to lead to the Austro-Prussia war and to Bismarck's great triumph. His annexation of the two duchies, long under Danish protection, showed Bismarck's diplomatic strategy at its best. It brought Prussia to the North sea and led to the building of the strategic Kiel canal across the neck of Jutland. Above all it forced Austria into actively suppor-

Opposite A cartoon from *Punch* 1866, starkly illustrating the bitterness between Austria and Prussia over the Schleswig-Holstein affair. Napoleon, ironically, was to gain nothing from the imminent Austro-Prussian war.

"WHEN ROGUES FALL OUT"—

Austria :—"GIVE IT ME ;—I WON IT !"

Prussia :—"I SHAN'T ! I'VE GOT IT !"

Nap (to Italy) :—"NOW, FRIEND, WHEN THE FIGHT BEGINS YOU CAN SEIZE WHAT YOU WANT !"

Above The King of Prussia, William I, leaves Berlin at the outbreak of the Austro–Prussian war of 1866.

ting Bismarck, even at the cost of its own exclusion from the German Confederation.

The facts, broadly, were that Austria and Prussia had signed the London agreement (1852) with Britain, France and Denmark. This recognized the two duchies as part of the Danish kingdom, but not subject to its laws. Schleswig was recognized as having a Danish speaking majority; Holstein was largely German-speaking. It was in fact a member of the German Confederation.

The future of the duchies was called in question after Schleswig had been formally incorporated into Denmark just before the death of the Danish King, Frederick VII. This broke the London Treaty. But what was going to happen to Holstein? Would it suffer the same fate? Feelings were running high, particularly among Germans.

In answer to the apparent threat to Holstein, the Confederation came out in support of the Duke of Augustenburg, a German prince, as the succeeding ruler of the duchy. But the move was opposed by both Prussia and Austria. They vetoed the resolution backing Augustenburg as it was a breach of the London agreement which they had both signed. Instead they decided, on Bismarck's suggestion, to act together and ignore the Confederation. To an outsider it seemed as if Bismarck was now favouring a conservative alliance with Austria within Germany.

On 1st February, 1864, Austrian and Prussian troops invaded Schleswig. By 18th April they were at the Danish frontier. No European power (least of all Britain which had half-promised help) came to her aid, and in October the new King of Denmark, Christian IX, was forced to sign away his rights over the duchies at the Treaty of Vienna.

Neither Austria nor Prussia showed any wish to go on co-operating over the duchies. Within a year the newly-formed Austrian-Prussian alliance had foundered. There were two main reasons for this. Firstly King William again demanded Prussian control of Germany north of the River Main, thus angering the Austrians. Secondly, Bismarck again refused to let Austria join the Zollverein. Was Bismarck deliberately trying to provoke Austrian retaliation?

Bismarck knew that the tide was running with him. He had also begun to sense a significant ground-swell of public feeling in his favour. Even some liberals were being won for the policy of "Blood and Iron". It would only be a matter of time before the Prussian tactics needled Austria into open conflict.

Bismarck's biggest headache during this period was to make sure that none of the "super-powers" would step in if Prussia went to war with Austria. Russia, because of the Polish affair, was certain to remain neutral. But what of France? Bismarck had to find out which way Napoleon III would jump.

In September, 1865, he went to meet Napoleon at

> "The Austrian war did not take place because the existence of Prussia was threatened or in obedience to public opinion or the will of the people. It was a war prepared with deliberation and recognised as necessary not to obtain territorial aggrandisement but to secure and establish Prussian hegemony in Europe." *Field Marshal von Molkte*

Above **Bismarck's coat of arms.**

Biarritz. Nothing was settled between them, though Bismarck came away convinced that Napoleon would not help Austria in the coming war. In any case Napoleon felt that Austria would win. Bismarck next turned to Italy.

In April 1866, after lengthy talks, the Italians agreed to support Prussia. They promised to attack Austria if war broke out within the next three months. In return, Italy was to be given Venetia.

The stage was set for the final confrontation. Bismarck had done all he could to isolate Austria by means of skilful diplomacy. All that remained to do was to convince William I of Austrian hostility. He did not have to wait long. On 1st June Austria turned over the task of deciding the future of Schleswig-Holstein to the Federal Diet. This marked the end of any previous Austro-Prussian understandings over the Schleswig-Holstein affair.

Bismarck retaliated by accusing the **Austrians** of "breach of contract," and formally demanding her exclusion from the Diet. But an Austrian counterclaim was laid against Prussia. The Diet voted against Prussia by 9 votes to 6. Bismarck then declared the Confederation dissolved. Immediate moves were made for military operations. Austria was apparently fighting to retain its senior position among the German states. Prussia wanted much more.

It took only seven weeks for the Prussian Army to force Austria to its knees.

Bismarck watched the fighting in the field-grey uniform of a general in the territorial reserve. It was the only military rank he held. He also had his first —though not the last—open clash with Prussian generals. It happened after the third week when the crushing defeat of the Austrians at Sadowa (Koeniggratz) left the road open to Vienna. Bismarck intervened to stop Vienna being taken by storm. He insisted that the troops should cross the River Danube lower down at Pressburg. It had never been Bismarck's aim to conquer Austria. He simply wanted to consolidate Prussia's control of northern Germany. War for Bismarck was only to be waged in the direst extremity, and then as briefly as possible. In any case, a longer war could have brought about Great Power intervention. Moderation in victory was the tactic with which to defeat Austria, without provoking direct French or Russian counter-moves.

The Austrian Emperor desperately appealed to France for help. But the most Napoleon III was prepared to do was to offer his services as mediator in the peace settlement.

Overleaf **The fierce and bloody battle at Sadowa, where Austria was utterly defeated and lost her supremacy within Germany.** *Below* **Bismarck (on the right) watches the fighting.**

Above **William I decorating the Crown Prince on the battlefield of Sadowa.**

Terms were agreed at the Treaty of Prague on 23rd August, 1866. All the conditions were Bismarck's, and all were accepted. Austria was to keep out of Germany; the old German confederation was to be dissolved. In its place, there was to be a new North German confederation under Prussian leadership. The south German states would have a separate national identity, Italy would get Venetia (the only territory Austria lost) and Schleswig was ceded to Prussia.

At the end of the day, Austria was still a Great Power; but she had been forced to acknowledge Prussia as her equal. North of the River Main the German states were bound together in a confederation which Prussia dominated.

France, which hoped to benefit from the Austro-Prussian war, got nothing. Indeed, as one Frenchman

said, "It is *we* who were beaten at Sadowa." As France could no longer play off the two German powers against one another she lost the leadership of Europe.

Furthermore, Napoleon III had aroused Bismarck's anger by obviously expecting a pay off in the form of territory, for acting as mediator. Five years later he got an even bigger shock when Bismarck trapped France into war with Prussia. After the Austrian adventure, Bismarck admitted: "Our linen was not always too clean." In 1870 it was even dirtier.

Everyone knew that the possibility of a Franco-Prussian war was a real danger. But the French refused to believe that their vaunted professional army could be matched by the Prussians, in spite of Sadowa. Besides, there had been intensive French diplomatic activity to put a line of protective buffer states round the country.

> "You cannot say he is a bad character. He kills his pleasure in other people by analysis and suspicion, by feeling annoyed when they contradict him, and by wearying of them." *Count Freidrich · von Holstein, Diaries*

Bismarck got malicious pleasure from exposing secret French moves. He became a specialist in exploiting the sensational press and the technique of the well-informed news "leak". He made a practice of feeding some of the great newspaper reporters of the time with "exclusive scoops".

Probably the most sensational exposure was evidence of French attempts to "buy up" Luxembourg. There was also evidence of French efforts to step up anti-Prussian feeling among the Rhineland states in the south.

France even tried to involve Belgium. When Bismarck published the draft of a French treaty which seemed to violate the old neutrality agreement over Belgium, British opinion swung sharply against France. It was strengthened with further reports that France also coveted a slice of Bavaria.

The immediate cause of the war with France was Bismarck's devious attempt to put up a "Hohenzollern candidate" for the throne of Spain after the Spanish revolution of 1868.

Bismarck's nominee was the young Prince Leopold von Hohenzollern-Signaringen. His father, a former Prussian premier, was all for the plan; the young Prince was a nonentity who did what he was told.

The French reacted violently. The whole thing was inflated into a Prussian conspiracy against the national interests of France. A counter diplomatic and press campaign of such violence was mounted that the Prince's father thought it wise to withdraw the claims of the Hohenzollern candidate. But not so Bismarck.

The French were equally suspicious of the motives behind the withdrawal. They distrusted everything to do with Bismarck. They took the withdrawal to be a tactical move, playing for time. Count Benedetti, the French Ambassador to Prussia, was told to pursue the matter and obtain categoric Prussian assurances that under no circumstances would further attempts be made to revive the proposal.

At the time, King William, the old Prussian monarch,

Below Prince Leopold von Hohenzollern, whose candidature for the Spanish throne helped pave the way for the Franco–Prussian war.

Left A dramatic, though inaccurate, illustration of the famous confrontation between Count Benedetti and William I at Ems. The fateful meeting in fact took place in the street.

was visiting a popular German watering spa called Ems. He was also to have private talks there with the Tsar of Russia. Bismarck, rather curiously, was not on the scene. He had stayed at home.

Count Benedetti adopted unusually crude undiplomatic means to fulfil his mission. He actually tried to buttonhole King William in the street. So rudely did he demand the assurances that the Prussian King broke off their conversation. A straight-forward report of the meeting by Heinrich Abeken, a German Foreign Office official, was telegraphed from Ems to Prince Bismarck at home.

> "I perceived in this extorted submission, an humiliation for Germany for which I did not desire to be responsible. This impression of a wound to our sense of national honour by the compulsory withdrawal so dominated me that I had already decided to announce my retirement at Ems. I considered the humiliation before France and her swaggering demonstrations as worse than that of Olmuitz for which the previous history on both sides and our want of preparation for war at that time will always be a valid excuse. I took it for granted that France would lay the Prince's renunciation to her accounts as a satisfactory success with the feeling that a threat of war, even though it had taken the form of an international insult and mockery, and though the pretext of war against Prussia had been dragged in by the head and shoulders, was enough to compel her to draw back even in a just cause . . . . I was very much depressed for I saw no means of repairing the corroding injury I dreaded to our national position . . . . I saw by that time that war was a necessity which could no longer avoid with humour . . ."
>
> *Otto von Bismarck. Reflections and Reminiscences* quoted by W. M. Simon, Germany in the Age of Bismarck. *Allen and Unwin. P 233*

The Ems telegram caused a sensation. As soon as Bismarck received it (he noted in his *Memoirs*) he saw Prussia facing another Olomouc humiliation. He was prepared to resign.

But this is not how the game was played out. Instead, the Iron Chancellor went off with the Ems telegraph in his pocket to dine with his friends, Field-Marshals von Moltke and von Roon. They all studied the note and waited for Bismarck's reaction. The Iron Chancellor satisfied their expectations by a dramatic demonstration of his skill at forcing diplomatic confrontations. As he reported in his *Memoirs,* he changed the whole emphasis of the telegram with a few strokes of his pencil. "I reduced the telegram by striking out a few words but without adding or altering anything."

As a result, the telegram read as though it was the Prussian King who had broken off all talks instead of merely interrupting a clumsy conversation in the street.

When Bismarck read out the edited message to his friends, von Moltke said "Now, it has a different ring. Before it sounded like a parley. Now it is a flourish in answer to a challenge."

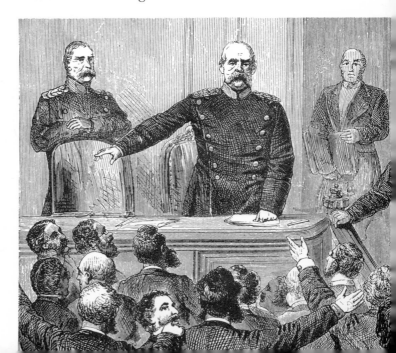

Right **Bismarck announces the outbreak of the Franco–Prussian war, which was to lead finally to the unification of Germany.**

Above **Prussian troops storm the outskirts of Paris towards the end of the Franco–Prussian war.**

Bismarck knew that the distribution of this edited message to the press and diplomatic corps would have "the effect of a red rag on a gallic bull." He wrote: "Fight we must, if we do not wish to act the part of being vanquished before the battle." As in 1866, Bismarck had skilfully provoked the enemy into attack. This time, however, he had all Germany behind him.

France declared war on 15th July, 1870. But the German army attacked first. The French were quickly and totally defeated. By 2nd September, the French army under General MacMahon and Napoleon III himself, was surrounded and capitulated at Sedan. On 27th October, the great French fort of Metz fell. Paris surrendered to the Prussians on 28th January, 1871.

An humiliating Peace Treaty was signed in the famous Hall of Mirrors in the Palace of Versailles outside Paris

Below The French army surrenders to the Prussians at Sedan in 1870. *Opposite top right* Otto von Bismarck "dictating" peace terms to the French. *Below* William I proclaimed Kaiser Wilhelm I, Emperor of Germany, at Versailles on 18th January, 1871.

on 28th February, 1871. Bismarck was still wearing the field-grey uniform of a reserve army general; a few days earlier he had fulfilled one of his supreme ambitions in the same Hall of Mirrors. He had crowned William the First of Prussia, the first Emperor of Germany. The unification of Germany (including the south German states) and the foundation of the German Reich with Kaiser Wilhelm I at its head had been created at last. There would be no further wars between the Great Powers in Bismarck's lifetime.

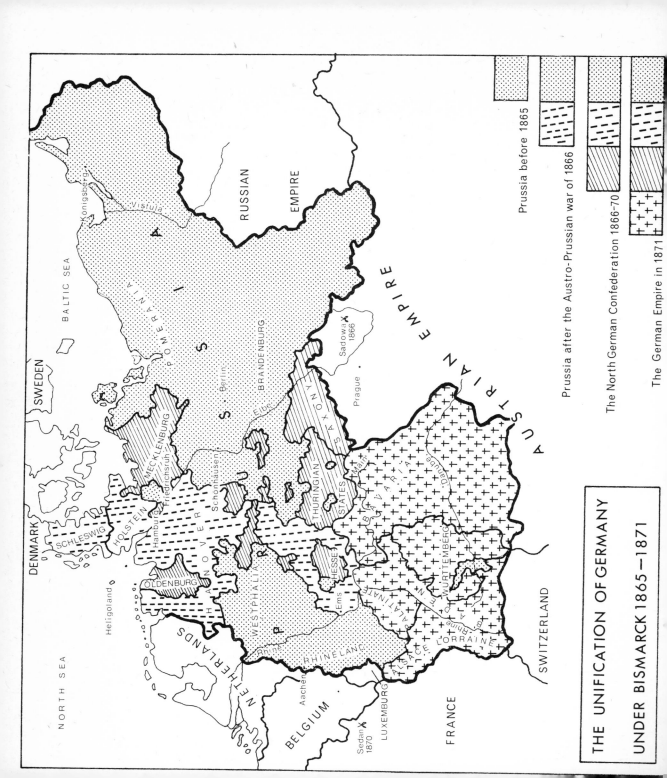

THE UNIFICATION OF GERMANY

UNDER BISMARCK 1865–1871

Prussia before 1865

Prussia after the Austro-Prussian war of 1866

The North German Confederation 1866–70

The German Empire in 1871

8 Total State

After 1871 the German Empire included Prussia, the kingdoms of Bavaria, Saxony and Wurttemberg, eighteen lesser states and Alsace-Lorraine. Suddenly, Germany was a super-power with an apparently invincible army.

Bismarck was in the saddle. He was Chancellor of Germany, the new Reich. He was also Minister-President and Foreign Minister of State of its most important constituent, Prussia. Later, he became Prussian Minister of Trade. He held all four posts until 1890 when he left office. He alone had the exclusive right of access to the Emperor.

The Chancellor had, inevitably, become a popular hero although those who knew him best were aware of his cynicism, ruthlessness and arrogance. But he had been created a prince; he was presented with large estates in Lauenburg, the small duchy that came in the Schleswig-Holstein packet, and he was the proud holder of the Iron Cross, 1st class.

The constitution of the new empire was virtually the same as the one drawn up for the North German confederation after the war with Austria. Most of the minor matters affecting the ordinary citizen were still dealt with by the individual states. The Reichstag or parliament was elected by universal, secret adult male suffrage. It had the right to debate the budget and fix the army estimates. But effective control was in the hands of the Bundesrat, the Federal Council which was the upper

"The old Emperor was not a great statesman but a man of sound judgement and a perfect gentleman. He was true to those who worked with him. I was deeply attached to him. He was a noble man, a sharp sword so to speak, with a short blade." *Otto von Bismarck on Wilhelm I.*

Below A symbolic statue showing Bismarck, represented as Germany's armourer, forging German unity.

house of parliament. Its representatives were nominated by the individual states, not by the people. Nor was it a true federation; Prussia, for example had a big block of 17 votes out of a total of 58. The Bundesrat could declare war, settle constitutional questions, and dissolve the Reichstag; its power was extremely wide-ranging. In command of the whole structure was the Chancellor—Otto von Bismarck—who was answerable only to the emperor.

Prince Otto von Bismarck had created the world's first modern Total State, the German Reich. Power was concentrated in his hands and, in the name of the Reich, Bismarck imposed his own policies on the German peoples. It was defined precisely by Heinrich von Treishke, a former liberal converted into a Bismarck fan. He wrote: "The core of the state is power. The state is not there for the citizen. It is an end in itself. Since the state is power, it can obviously draw into its sphere of influence all human activities . . ."

To complete the unification of the Reich and to build a strong centralized authority—this was Bismarck's aim in the 1870s. It meant legislation and so he co-operated with the National Liberal Party, the majority grouping in Parliament. Together they built the new empire.

The army and the civil service, the railway, postal and legal systems were unified. A common coinage was introduced. German laws and customs were imposed on foreign minority groups, such as the French in Alsace and the Poles in Prussia. Only two political parties put up any opposition to Bismarck's concept of the state —the Social Democratic Party and the Catholic Centre Party. The S.D.P. were as yet not strong enough to pose a threat, but the Catholics, Bismarck decided, were antinational and therefore dangerous. He took steps in 1873 to curb their political influence by embarking on a *Kulturkampf* or "struggle for civilization". The *Kulturkampf* was enforced with a series of "May Laws" which came into force between 1873–79. These entailed state control of education, state control of the appointment of clergy and the dissolution of religious orders.

However, far from weakening the Catholic Centre Party, the anti-clerical laws of the *Kulturkampf* actually helped the Catholics to increase their representation in Parliament. At least a third of the German empire (mostly the states of the River Main) was Catholic and all resented Bismarck's action. It seemed to them that Bismarck was imposing Prussian autocracy on Catholics and minority groups alike. From 1879 onwards the failure of this policy was clear even to Bismarck; he began to relax the May Laws.

The ending of the *Kulturkampf* was also a political necessity. In the parliamentary elections of 1878 the Social Democrats sharply increased their representation in the Reichstag. Bismarck needed to find a way of undermining their power. He could make no use of the National Liberals—he had broken with them the year before over the question of introducing economic measures.

Above Isolated and aloof, The Chancellor listens to a speech in the German Reichstag.

Above **The all-powerful Chancellor surrounded by deputies, most of whom he scorned and despised, in the Reichstag.**

Bismarck's solution was typically adroit and autocratic. As a first step, he demanded protective tariffs to safeguard German trade, so wooing the Catholic Centre Party which had been campaigning for just such a measure. This gave Bismarck the support of the Catholics in his coming fight with the Social Democrats. It also meant that revenue could be raised through customs duties independently of the Reichstag.

The results for German industry were sensational. Some years later, in 1919, the British economist John Maynard Keynes wrote: "Germany was not founded so much on blood and iron as on iron and steel."

The statistical record was impressive. There were huge increases in every field of production. In the 1880s Germany doubled its output of steel and nearly trebled its coal production. By 1914 coal production had risen by more than 162 million tons since 1871. Pig iron production had gone up by nearly 14 million metric tons.

The huge industrial complex of the Ruhr was developing on the basis of Westphalian coal, and the basic ores of Luxembourg and Lorraine.

Germany had run far ahead of its European rivals in building its chemical and electrical industries. Her rail system had been extended by thousands of kilometres. Her shipping had also moved onto all the world's major trading routes.

New problems appeared on the horizon. The speed of economic progress brought social tensions, and population problems. The rural population was sucked into the towns. The previous 60:40 ratio between country and town was almost exactly reversed. There were increasing housing problems, slums, poverty, unemployment and class bitterness. The heaviest burdens fell on the poor.

In response to the horrors of the industrial revolution, the Social Democratic Party and trade union movement attracted widespread support. To Bismarck the Social Democrats were a grave threat to the stability of the state. He was also suspicious of the opposition's "internationalism" and flatly opposed any suggestion that the private ownership of land and property should be abolished. Bismarck, however, was perfectly willing to accept the right to work and state aid to protect jobs. These were acceptable ideas—threats to the stability of the state were not. He had to solve the problem.

Characteristically he went for a solution which made him appear the champion of social reform. He sought to outflank the opposition, or the left, by a policy of apparent "state socialism." After a series of dramatic confrontations with the opposition (including the passing of the Exemplary Law in 1879 which outlawed the Social Democratic Party) Bismarck made his biggest contribu-

> "I never ask if something is popular only if it is reasonable and justifiable."
> *Otto von Bismarck*

tion to social legislation by bringing in the compulsory social insurance acts he had talked about years before in 1866 with Ferdinand Lasalle, one of the earliest pioneers of socialist thought. By themselves they would have assured Bismarck a place in history. The three Acts, on Old Age Pension, Factory Accidents and Health, were introduced in 1881 but it was 1884 before they became law. Had the great conservative become a genuine social reformer? Whatever the real motives for the Chancellor's policy, the fact remains that Bismarck's state welfare legislation was the first of its kind anywhere in the world. It was to be taken up by other European countries. Later Bismarck was even talking of the need for a form of insurance against unemployment.

Bismarck probably believed sincerely in his programme of social welfare, but he certainly had ulterior motives for introducing it. Above all, he wanted the workers to become pawns of the state. The reduction of their independence meant, inevitably, they would become more reliant on Bismarck and so strengthen his overall political position. It seemed to be a fair balance. The social legislation, like all Bismarck's political moves, was shrewdly produced when it was likely to be of most benefit to him. It was not in his character to tie himself to any one cause; now that he needed parliamentary support he wooed the politicians. He had learned the tricks of political haggling at horse fairs. Up to 1878 he worked with the National Liberals since it suited his purpose. He dropped them, once they had outgrown their usefulness and went fishing for the Centre Party using protective tariffs and social reform as bait. As in foreign policy, he balanced opposing forces against one another. All were ruthlessly manipulated for his own ends.

Opposite The industrial revolution in Germany caused much distress and suffering which Bismarck's social legislation tried to ameliorate: *Above* Slums in Berlin built under the shadow of a factory. *Below* Some of the homeless poor queue up for a night's lodging.

EVERYBODY'S FRIEND!

9 Honest Broker

By 1871 Bismarck occupied a unique position in European politics. He was leader of a new Great Power; he was the imperial Chancellor and Prime Minister of Prussia. He had overthrown Austrian supremacy in Germany, and realized Prussian ambitions. It was now his concern to maintain the *status quo* between the Great Powers (Russia, France, Austria and Germany) and to prevent any further wars which would upset the balance of power.

To Bismarck, the best way of ensuring peace was to make Germany the pivot of a European balance of power. If he could keep on good terms with all the other European powers, forcing them to rely on the potential weight of Germany's military might, he could be the effective arbiter of the European situation.

Two major problems, however, always remained at issue. The first was the question of German security against France; the second, that of Austrian and Russian rivalry in the Balkans and the eastern end of the Mediterranean. (Now it is known as the Middle East. In those days they called it the Near East.) Both in 1875 and 1887 Bismarck created imaginary fears in Germany of another Franco-Prussian war for domestic reasons but mostly to try to isolate France from the other powers. To attack Germany France needed allies. Bismarck was determined to undermine their confidence. In 1887 he even convinced the Tsar that a Russian alliance with France would result in her attacking Germany, bringing republicanism and revolution in Germany.

"If I am not certain who is the first diplomat in Europe, I am certain Lord Beaconsfield is the second." *Otto von Bismarck*

Austro-Russian rivalry in the Near East was a trickier problem, and one which dogged Bismarck for the rest of his career. Above all, he wanted to avoid any direct confrontation between these two powers. A war in the Balkans would force Germany to take sides, and Bismarck had no wish to get involved. In a famous phrase he declared that the Balkans contained "no German interest worth the bones of a Pomeranian musketeer."

In 1871, the year following the Franco-Prussian war, Bismarck worked to recreate the so-called "Holy Alliance" of Russia, Austria and Germany, the *Dreikaiserbund*. It was a conspicuously conservative alliance implicitly aimed at isolating republican France. As always, Bismarck was seeking to kill two birds with one stone. In 1873 he obtained assurances that in event of an unprovoked attack by one, the other two powers would mutually support each other. But though Austria was firmly committed to this ingenious diplomatic device, it was not firmly binding on either Russia or Germany. Spurred on by renewed fighting in the Balkans Bismarck took up the role of "Honest Broker".

Bismarck found himself in a position to play the role of arbitrator because his two powerful eastern allies, Russia and Austria, were threatening each other over the Balkans. The Austrians were challenging the Russians for organizing a pan-Slav movement against them among the Serbians, Croats and Montenegrins of what is now Yugoslavia. The Austrians claimed that this broke an earlier convention defining respective spheres of interest, drawn up by Bismarck at Reichstadt (1876).

The Russians were also accused of grabbing more Balkan territory. After Turkey was ousted from huge areas of the Balkans in the war with Russia (1877–78) she was forced to hand over what is now Bulgaria, under the Treaty of San Stefano (1879). The new Bulgarian state had been set up under Russian protection with the Tsar's nephew, Prince Alexander von Battenberg, on the throne. The Austrians were suspicious and hostile. They feared more Russian expansion.

smarck. Schwaloff. Onbril.　Gortschakoff　Russell　Salisbury　Beaconsfield Haymerle Karolyi Andrassy　Bismarck　Waddington　St.Valier.　Déprez
　Dr Busch.　　　　　　　　　　　　　　　　　　　　Hohenlohe　　Radowitz　　Bülow.　　　　　　　　Corti
　　　　　　　　　　　Mouy.　　　　　　　　　　　　　Sadullah Bey.　Mehemed-Ali. Caratheodory　de Launay. Curto-Passi.

ololyp.Jnstitut.　Robert Prager C. Seydelstr. 29.　　　　　　　　　　　　　　　　　№ 250. Gesetzlich Geschützt. 1878.

Britain was involved because of the supposed threat to British imperial interests of any Russian advance on Constantinople. A wild Russian sweep to the north west passes of India was feared. Russian expansionist moves were taking place in Central Asia. Also what was going to happen to the short cut to India through the recently purchased Suez canal? An emotional storm was whipped up in Britain over this alleged threat.

Above **Bismarck (standing in front of the window) in his role of "Honest Broker" and arbiter of the fortunes of Europe presiding over the peace congress in Berlin in 1878.**

All the major powers accepted Bismarck's offer to mediate at a peace congress in Berlin in 1878. The British Prime Minister, Benjamin Disraeli, was quite willing for Bismarck to safeguard British interests in the Near East, if this could be done. As it happened Bismarck and Disraeli liked each other at once. Both had climbed "to the top of the greasy pole" of politics; both were realists with qualities in common.

The Congress of Berlin was a tremendous success, mainly because agreement had already been reached between Russia and Britain, and Russia and Austria. Other private business was quickly settled by Bismarck behind the scenes. Disraeli returned home crying "Peace with Honour"; the Austrians and Russians seemed happy with the complicated settlements they had ratified. Bismarck, though he thoroughly enjoyed acting as the elder statesman of Europe, was less enthusiastic, believing the meeting had only "papered over the cracks."

Indeed Russia felt badly treated at the Congress, and Tsar Alexander was not slow to blame Bismarck for an imagined loss of prestige at Berlin. He wrote to the Kaiser complaining of the way Russia had been pressurized into giving up some of its gains made under the treaty of San Stefano. The truth was that Bismarck was a better diplomat than the Russian Emperor.

Signs of Bismarck's awareness of the delicacy of German-Russian relations were given by the way he started looking for allies elsewhere. He even made advances to Disraeli for some sort of "arrangement". But he got little encouragement.

The British Prime Minister was suspicious of the Chancellor's double-dealing. It was too much like diplomatic cardsharping, he told Lord Salisbury. And he had given Queen Victoria a hint of his suspicions in the characteristically superior letter he wrote her from Berlin during the Congress.

"I sat on the right of Prince Bismarck, and I could listen to his Rabelaisian monologues and endless revela-

Opposite **Bismarck and Benjamin Disraeli (Lord Beaconsfield)** conduct a private discussion away from the conference table in Berlin in 1878. Both statesmen respected each other enormously.

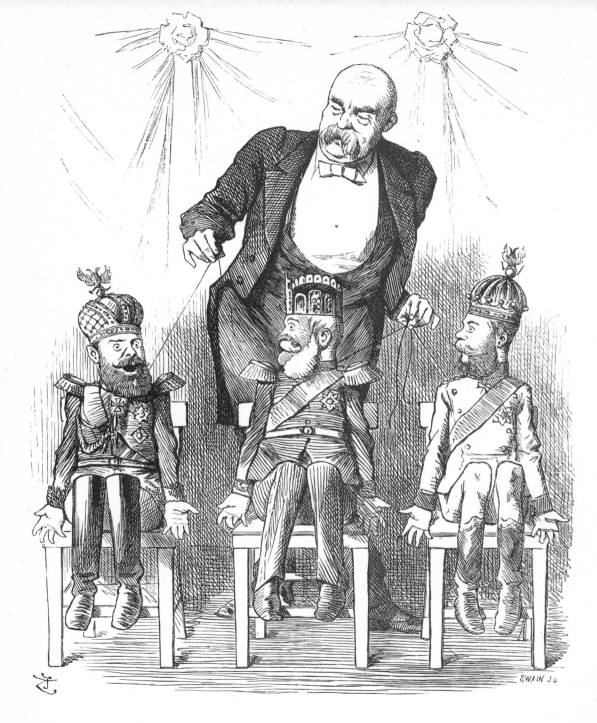

THE THREE EMPERORS;

OR, THE VENTRILOQUIST OF VARZIN!

tion of things he ought not to mention," he wrote to the Queen. "He impressed on me never to trust Princes or countries; that his illness was not, as people supposed, brought on by the French war, but by the horrible conduct of his sovereign. In the archives of his family remain the documents, royal letters which accuse him, after all his services, of being a traitor. He went on in such a vein that I was obliged to tell him that instead of encountering the "duplicity" which he said was universal among sovereigns, I served one who was the soul of candour and justice and whom all her Ministers loved."

Bismarck inquired in London, what would be Britain's reaction if Germany became involved in difficulties in the Near East? Disraeli replied that he would ensure the neutrality of France and Italy. Bismarck commented, "Is that all?" Afterwards, when Russia suggested a revival of the *Dreikaiserbund* in 1881 he dropped any further attempt to make Britain a German ally.

Instead Bismarck rushed into another a treaty with Austria in 1879. Again his major concern was to prevent a war in the Balkans between Russia and Austria. With the promise of German security he hoped to convince the Austrians that they had no quarrel with Russia. Similarly he hoped Russia would think twice before attacking an Austrian-German alliance.

Such a policy was a flat contradiction of his earlier days, when he referred to Austria as "a worm-eaten old galleon". The truth was that Bismarck was old and conservative. Twenty-five years earlier he would have set about the reconstruction of the Balkans with the same fervour that made him redraw the map of Western Europe. To get his way he fought his last great battle with William I. In opposing the Austrian alliance the Emperor used all Bismarck's old arguments—the need of friendship with Russia to isolate France, the traditional amity of the Hohenzollerns with the Tsar. Yet Bismarck in the end got the old Emperor's consent. As in all things, Bismarck had the stronger will. He *had* to get his own way.

Opposite Punch's **illustration of how Bismarck manipulated the** *Dreikaiser-bund* **to bolster his** *Pax Germanicus* **and prevent full-scale war in the Balkans.**

From this moment on Bismarck had more absolute power than ever before. He manipulated the Reichstag despite the complaints of the opposition parties. He kept free of criticism from the Emperor. There were no threats to resign, no more confessions that he was weary of office. He ruled alone without colleagues. In 1885 he made his son Herbert Secretary of State. Herbert was the only person he trusted. He had contempt for all other politicians, both German and foreign.

The 1880s were the last decade of Bismarck's reign. Despite his irascibility and contempt for others, his health had much improved. He lost weight, slept better and appeared fit and upright. The tottering old man of the 1870s was replaced by a rejuvenated Bismarck. In the Reichstag he spoke not for one party but for Germany and her interests. Yet Bismarck really knew very little of what was really motivating the German people. He did not read any new literature; he never met the leading thinkers of his day; he knew nothing of industrial conditions. Life inside Germany was a closed book.

All his interest centred on retaining the miracle of a Europe at peace under a system which he had conjured into being.

Left **Bismarck conferring with the President of Saxony in the German Reichstag. Fit and seemingly rejuvenated Bismarck completely dominated both the Reichstag and William I in the 1880s.**

10 No Colony Man

Bismarck always insisted that he did not really want colonies. But in the 1880s he used the growing rivalries between the main colonial powers, notably Britain and France, to wangle his way into the imperial game. He was now out to isolate Britain even by courting the French, particularly if colonies could be used to achieve this end. Moreover, if France was preoccupied with her own colonial expansion, she was less likely to constitute a threat to German security.

It was easy enough to stand on the sidelines cheering on troublemakers. Bismarck had done this in 1880 when he supported France against Britain over the occupation of Morocco. A year later he was setting Italy against France by encouraging France to occupy Tunisia. The Italians were understandably perturbed. There were 10,000 Italian settlers in Libya, then generally seen as a strategic sphere of Italian interest though the territory was nominally under the Ottoman Empire.

The Italians turned to Germany and Austria. They came into Bismarck's "Triple Alliance" and joined Austria and Germany. Again this reflected Bismarck's anti-British stance; it meant that both Austria and Italy, whom Britain hoped would combat Russian influence in the Balkans and French influence in the Mediterranean respectively, were lost to Germany.

The momentum of its own economic growth was bound to force Germany into active competition in the colonial scramble. Overseas markets were an absolute

> "Colonial policy is not caused by Generals and Privy Councillors but by Trading Houses and Commercial Travellers." *Otto von Bismarck*

necessity to absorb surplus production and stimulate new growth; so were raw materials, both as fuel for factories and food for the population. Finally, overseas colonies would be some compensation to the Hamburg merchants for the loss of free trade brought about by the protective tariffs.

Big shipping and trading interests in Hamburg, Bremen and elsewhere had been pressing for a more active colonial policy since the 1860s. Prospectors in the field, notably traders and missionaries, had opened up centres and posts in south west, central and east Africa long before Bismarck felt the need to change his policy. They were clamouring for diplomatic and military protection.

A more aggressive Association for German Colonisation had taken over in 1881 from the less militant *Kolonialverein*.

Angra Pequena, better known as German South West Africa (now called Namibia), is a bleak stretch of territory north-west of Cape Colony (a British possession); this became the starting-point of the real scramble for Africa. Bismarck was obviously piqued at the failure of Disraeli's administration to recognize Angra Pequena as German territory; or perhaps they were merely puzzled at the way the Chancellor had also tentatively suggested he might even be prepared to withdraw if Britain ceded the North Sea territory of Heligoland in exchange?

Whatever the motive, Germany suddenly proclaimed its annexation of the territory. It was quickly followed by demands for international recognition of German protectorates over Togoland and the Cameroons in West Africa, and Tanganyika in the East. Agents of the rival powers were literally racing to get to new tribal territory on the basis of first come first served. One group of Germans put in a formal claim after arriving only five days before the British.

What was behind the Chancellor's apparent determination to block a British monopoly of all available African territory south of the Sahara?

THE "IRREPRESSIBLE" TOURIST.

B-SM-RCK. "H'M!—HA!—WHERE SHALL I GO NEXT?"

It was not simply a matter of cash returns. Nor did continuing Anglo-French colonial friction have so much to do with it. The fact was that Bismarck was increasingly conscious of the internal domestic situation he was likely to face when the old Kaiser died. Wilhelm I had been born in 1797. He would be succeeded by the Crown Prince and his English wife, the eldest daughter of Queen Victoria. They were clearly pro-British. Also, although there was little external evidence to support it, they were said to be much more liberal than the Old Kaiser.

Bismarck reckoned he would not only have to face a revival led by the National Liberals, but also more and more pressure for parliamentary procedures more in line with the House of Commons than the Reichstag.

To prepare for this, Bismarck may well have deliberately courted reactionary, aggressively imperialist politicians, in order to stack the Reichstag with members hostile to the new Kaiser and his wife. It would be far easier to do this if he could generate tension over alleged Anglo-German hostility when the time was ripe.

It was typical of Bismarck, that as Anglo-German tensions multiplied over colonial affairs, he should start fishing for possible new working arrangements with the British government—even secret treaties.

He did not get any. But he made a last effort to block British expansion in Africa, by making overtures to France over the Congo. He persuaded the French to join him in calling a conference in Britain over reported atrocities in the Congo rubber plantations. But it turned out, when it came to the point, that Britain was more concerned with blocking French expansion in the area.

As a result King Leopold of the Belgians skilfully used the divisions between the powers, and Bismarck's suspicions of Britain, to win control of the Congo for himself.

Almost simultaneously, Bismarck's brief attempt to cultivate a new relationship with France collapsed with the political defeat of Jules Ferry, the chief architect of French colonization.

"The Chancellor's humours are as changeable as those of the French Assembly's, and you can never be certain that he will not try to levy a sort of diplomatic blackmail." *Lord Salisbury*

A new wave of anti-German suspicion swept France. The old Chancellor was again forced to play politics in Europe to defend his so-called *Pax Germanicus*.

Above A dramatic reconciliation: Bismarck (standing in the carriage) meets William II (on horseback), four years after Bismarck's fall from power.

11 The Battenberg Business

On 3rd March, 1888, Bismarck came to the Reichstag to announce the death of William I. Bismarck was weeping as he made his formal statement, partly from grief at the old man's death, partly because he foresaw his own hold on power stipping. Bismarck had had major battles with the Emperor, all of which he had won. Now, just when he had gained complete mastery over William, who had come to see Bismarck as the champion of democracy against parliamentary revolution, the old man had died.

William's son Frederick III was the new Emperor. He was already dying from cancer of the throat when he ascended the throne. In the event he was to rule for only nine months. Nevertheless, Bismarck was determined to impress on his new master that he was still in control, that his will was law.

He found an excuse with the proposed marriage between Alexander von Battenberg, Prince of Bulgaria, and Viktoria, daughter of the new Kaiser and Kaiserina. The Kaiserina was also Viktoria, and the eldest daughter of Queen Victoria, Empress of Britain and India. Bismarck vetoed the match and made it a resignation matter. He told Frederick III that such an alliance would wreck what was left of Germany's friendship with Russia. The chief reason was the violent antagonism now being shown by Battenberg to his Russian sponsors. He had been put on the Bulgarian throne in 1879 by his uncle, the Tsar of Russia, but had refused to follow Russian policy. He was ambitious and adventurous and

Opposite Otto von Bismarck announces the death of his master, William I, from the steps of the Reichstag on 3rd March, 1888.

Below Prince Alexander von Battenberg, whose marriage to Viktoria, daughter of Frederick III, Bismarck strenuously opposed.

reckoned he could play a game of his own.

The Chancellor was convinced that Queen Victoria and British imperial strategists were behind the Prince. The move also tended to confirm the old warhorse's view of how domestic politics were to develop in Germany after the Kaiser's death. Also, he did not like the House of Battenberg-Hesse, of which Alexander was a member. They had stood out, with Saxony and Bavaria, against his unification policy, and Prussian hegemony. The future Earl Mountbatten, years later, was to claim that Battenberg anti-Prussian attitudes had been a major factor behind his father's loyalty to Britain during the Great War (1914–18). (He was talking about Prince Louis Battenberg who had served in the Royal Navy as an Admiral and changed his name to Mountbatten during the Great War.)

The Royal marriage was first mooted in August 1884, "in absolute secrecy," according to Frederick von Holstein. "The Crown Princess is counting on the Queen of England to overcome opposition," he wrote in his diary. "The Chancellor is very much opposed. He has declared he will resign if there is any more talk of a Bulgarian marriage. If that happened he could assume no further responsibility for the foreign policy of the Reich."

There could be no question of putting 45 million Germans at risk for the sake of one, it was stated. Bismarck went much further in talks with the Kaiser. He warned him that Queen Victoria was ready to intervene personally. A visit of the Prince of Wales to the Reich might pave the way, he suggested. The Old Kaiser reacted violently: "She can do what she likes with her Princess Beatrice, but she had better leave my Princess alone!"

There were endless family rows, confrontations and recriminations as the Crown Princess persisted in her campaign. Nobody seems to have shown much interest in what the young Princess felt. In one emotional scene, reported by von Holstein, the Crown Princess burst into tears and flounced out of the room shouting, "You will be the death of my poor child!"

Above Bismarck the beer-drinker. Until very late in life Bismarck was proud of the prodigious amounts of beer and food he consumed.

Left **Prince Alexander von Battenberg carried in triumph by his supporters following his countercoup in Bulgaria in 1886.**

Bismarck shouted after her, "I cannot plunge my country into war on account of your ambitions!"

The domestic situation was beginning to reach public ears. Both sides were obviously inspiring rival press campaigns. A scurrilous pamphlet was circulating about Queen Victoria's alleged intrigues against the Reich.

In August 1886, Battenberg was kidnapped by Russian officers, and a provisional revolutionary government was installed at Sofia. A countercoup followed. But Battenberg did not withdraw his abdication. Instead he came hotfoot to Berlin. He needed money and a job. Bismarck no longer had grounds for opposition to the match so long as Battenberg had enough money to keep his wife in the condition to which she was accustomed. He did not care whether Russia or England footed the bill.

The Chancellor, as always, still suspected Battenberg's motives, as well as those of the younger Royals behind him. He had some justification. It became clear that powerful forces were sponsoring the Prince when the Kaiser made him a General in an elite Prussian regiment.

Von Holstein wrote: "The Chancellor is obsessed with Battenberg. He has written a scurrilous report branding him as a coward and God knows what else. He has sent it to the Crown Prince, and afterwards intends to publish it."

But Bismarck's instincts were right. The young man was hoping for a big job. The suggestion being canvassed was Governor of Alsace-Lorraine. Such a move could even lead to him personally challenging the old man for the Chancellorship. Bismarck reported to the Kaiser:

"All parties and individuals willing for the overthrow of the existing order realized with unerring instinct that Prince Alexander with his connections with influential circles in Germany and England could, under certain conditions, be used as a figure head. The preliminary basis for their calculation is, first, the rank of General held by the Prince in the Prussian army, and, second, his royal relatives. Any man in that position equipped as well with the outstanding qualities of heart and mind which the press attributes to Prince Alexander, justifiably becomes a candidate for an exalted position . . ."

The Kaiser noted his "entire agreement with the threatening nature of the Prince of Bulgaria's behaviour" on the cover of the document.

The question of the Battenberg marriage became academic. In April 1888, the Kaiser had a last interview with Bismarck over the affair. It was agreed the marriage could go ahead as a morganatic affair. But somehow it never did. Alexander became the Count of Hartenau. He died in 1893.

Below Bismarck, seated on the right, presides over a family gathering. Herbert, his son and his Secretary of State, is nearest the camera.

12 Dropping the Pilot

Bismarck's long lease on power finally ended in March 1890. He had been in almost complete control of the affairs of the Reich for twenty-eight years, and in state service for forty years. He had survived political intrigues and several assassination attempts.

The Prince was now a rich man. He had received huge cash prizes for his achievements. On his 71st birthday he was given some £270,000 raised by public subscription. Some of it went to charity, but he was also able to reclaim the old family estate of Schoenhausen. He had already headed the Honours list voted by the Assembly after the Austrian victory. It included another cash payment of £60,000. He also had a huge wooded estate and farm land at Friedrichsruh in his Duchy of Lauenburg. His favourite home was at Varzin, a village not far from Berlin. He had always spent much time away from his office, complaining of aches and pains, and the Chancellor's office had frequently been shifted, complete with staff and files, to the village.

Now he was old, tired, increasingly bad-tempered and resentful of opposition and of the rising generation. His eclipse was inevitable. It came quickly after the accession to the throne of the young Emperor Wilhelm II, the future "Kaiser Bill" of the First World War.

Bismarck had seldom bothered to hide his scorn for the young Kaiser. He regarded him as a brash, callow, intemperate and irresponsible youth. "He makes so many enemies he doesn't need friends," he told a confidant.

Opposite Old but desperate to retain his grip on power, Bismarck relaxes with his dogs at his home at Varzin.

"I cannot stand him much longer. He wants even to know whom I see and has spies set to watch those who come and go out of my office. It comes of an over-estimation of himself and of his inexperience of affairs that can lead to no good. He is much too conceited. He is simply longing with his whole heart to be rid of me in order that he may govern alone (with his own genius) and cover himself with glory. He does not want the old mentor any longer but only a docile tool. But I cannot make genuflections nor crouch under the table like a dog. He wants to break with Russia and yet he has not the courage to . . . *Otto von Bismarck on Wilhelm II.*

Above **William II ("Kaiser Bill" of World War I) who was responsible for sacking Bismarck.**

Wilhelm in turn had no confidence in Bismarck. His personal dislike of the old Chancellor was coupled to his political prejudices. These had been obvious even before his grandfather had died. He had put himself at the head of the war party and the new generation. These included some of the most forceful and expansionist elements in German industry and commerce. He had also picked up some of Bismarck's former advisers and colleagues. Many of these had become bitter and resentful of their cavalier treatment at the hands of the Chancellor. Among these "lost friends" was Friedrich von Holstein.

The Kaiser had made no secret of his intention to rid himself of the Chancellor once and for all. "I'll give the old man six months before I take complete charge," he boasted in his favourite officers' mess. "There is only one master in this country, and I am it!"

In fact it took William II a whole year to unseat Bismarck. The election of 1890 paved the way. Bismarck fought the campaign on a cry of the dangers of socialism. He failed to carry the country with him. The Liberals, Socialists and Centrists secured an anti-Bismarck majority in the Reichstag. Clearly support for Bismarck was on the wane.

According to the imperial constitution the Chancellor must resign if he lost the confidence of the Emperor. Bismarck simply ignored this. He would have to be pushed to the brink before he would retire. He seemed to be grimly hanging on to office as he said in 1888, "I shall refuse to sign any letter of resignation, I shall cling to my chair and not go even if they try to throw me out."

William II did all he could to hasten the end. To irritate Bismarck and to gain the support of his subjects, he began pandering to the German people by expressing sympathy with anti-Bismarck views and with the attitudes of industrial workers. His action outraged Bismarck. The Kaiser's action seemed calculated to undermine his personal authority. Bismarck decided to force a confrontation. He circulated a minute reminding Ministers, and provincial governments, that by virtue of a long-standing royal command all requests for audience of the monarch must be cleared through the Chancellor.

The Kaiser took Bismarck's action as an open personal challenge to himself, and a public insult to Hohenzollern dignity. In a towering rage the Kaiser drove down to Bismarck's estate. It was early in the morning of 20th March, 1890. The old man was called out of bed and asked to account for his action.

The Chancellor refused to back down. Instead he wrote out his resignation, as the Kaiser intended him to do. No attempt was made, this time, to persuade him to withdraw it.

On 29th March, with a guard of honour and full ceremonial trappings, Bismarck boarded the train for his estate at Varzin. As the train left Berlin, Bismarck said, "A state funeral with full honours."

Isolated at Varzin, Bismarck summed up his life, "I am 75, my wife is still with me, I have not lost any of my children. I always believed I should die in service. I have been at my post for twenty-eight years, in sickness and in health. I really do not know what I should do now, for I feel in better health than in years past." Nothing was said of his achievements, no hint of his fears for the future. His career seemed to have saved him from boredom and that was all.

But Bismarck did not quite grasp the fact that he was out in the cold. He dreamed of being revenged on his enemies and being recalled into the highest office. He did all he could to make his departure as difficult as possible. He would not advise his successors, he took all his official papers to Varzin with him and also pressurized his son Herbert into resigning from his post.

At Varzin, Bismarck languished. Nobody came to visit him, either on a social visit or to ask his political advice. In retaliation Bismarck began dictating his memoirs, which were to be a grand survey of his years in power. But the book itself was not published until after the Great War. Bismarck was not concerned with the truth.

"Our policy with its crisscross of commitments resembles the tangle of lines at a railway station. The chief pointsman thinks he can click everything into proper place and hopes particularly, that the greater the confusion, the more indispensable he is."
von Holstein Diaries.

"I feel I may venture the opinion that the Prince's policy, throughout his reign now offers a striking example of political ineptitude. With, one may say, an almost childish wilfulness he followed one after the other, mutually contradictory promptings of his personal ambition and never went far enough along any of the paths chosen to be able to convince himself for certain it was mistaken. But his worst fault, in the field of statesmanship, is his lack of loyalty and reliability. A politician who has lost his reputation in this respect can find no one to believe in him and that means the end of his career . . . ." *Further extract from report of Reich Chancellor Otto von Bismarck, to Kaiser Wilhelm I. German Foreign Ministry files. 20.9.1886.*

His aim was to write history as he wished it to be seen. Similarly in his writing for newspapers he constantly harped on the inadequacy of his successors and the doom which would befall Europe if his system was destroyed. He still saw himself as indispensable.

Abroad, in fact, there was little change. Bismarck's aim of friendship with Russia was continued. The break only came in 1914 when Germany supported Austria's attack on Serbia which helped precipitate the First World War. At home, no Bismarckian party appeared to keep his ideas alive. The truth was that Bismarck was too old; he wanted to stay still, to keep life as it was. The younger generation wanted new achievements, a new "world policy," social reform and a great Germany with Austria.

Bismarck's dramatic reconciliation never came. In 1894 William II made peace with him, but never asked his advice on matters of policy. Above all he neglected Bismarck's belief that "Germany should keep within her boundaries." In 1914, the fragile peace in Europe which Bismarck created and nurtured for nineteen years was eventually shattered. By then Otto von Bismarck was dead.

But Germany's debt to Bismarck remained. He had, above all, succeeded in giving it an identity, structure and unity. Erick Marck, one of his best biographers, wrote: "Bismarck educated us, perhaps too exclusively, to the realities of power, work and practical issues."

World interest in the Chancellor was shown by the astonishing range of the bibliography dealing with his work and personality. By 1907, there were more than 3,800 books on Bismarck in addition to his own huge output of memoirs and correspondence.

Louis Snyder, one of his American biographers, summed him up in *Blood and Iron Chancellor*: "He was one of history's unique personalities. Huge, portentous, like some vast monolith from the living rock of the earth. There was little stilted or dry about him. He had one of the best brains of his day. He worked like Richelieu; he had the girth of Falstaff and the split per-

"He usually began by taking the wrong road. But in the end he always allowed himself to be put straight again. His knowledge of affairs was limited and he was slow in comprehending anything new." *Bismarck's Memoirs, edited Busch*

Opposite "Dropping the Pilot": the famous cartoon first illustrated in *Punch* showing Bismarck finally ousted from power by William II.

sonality of Hamlet. He seemed as much an extension of his nation's personality for Germany, as Winston S. Churchill was for Britain in World War Two.''

Names in the Game

Alexander II (1818–81) Tsar of Russia, admirer of Bismarck, closely allied to Prussia.

Allexander III (1845–94) Tsar of Russia, switched Russia's support from Germany to France; related by marriage to Battenberg's (later Mountbattens) of Hesse-Darmstadt.

Bismarck, Prince Otto Eduard Leopold, Duke of Lauenberg (1815–98) Reich Chancellor, Foreign Minister of German Empire.

Disraeli, Benjamin, 1st Earl of Beaconsfield (1804–81), founder of modern British Tory party; purchased Suez Canal (1875), attended Congress of Berlin (1878).

Franz Joseph, Emperor of Austria, King of Hungary (1838–1916). Dominant monarch of the German Confederation until Austria's defeat by Bismarck, 1866.

Hohenzollern-Signaringen, Prince Leopold. Son of Prince Charles Anthony, Prime Minister of Prussia, married sister of the King of Portugal. The "Prussian Candidate" for the throne of Spain (1866) provoking the Franco-Prussian War.

Von Holstein, Count Friedrich (1837–1909). Bismarck's assistant and critic. Warned it was diplomatically "incompatible" to keep a diary, he posted loose pages of notes and records to his cousin Ida von Stulpnagel, for safe keeping.

Marx, Karl (1818–85), founder of modern economic-social theory, historian and contemporary of Bismarck at Berlin University. Launched *Communist Manifesto* (1848), propagandist of the concept of international socialism.

Von Molkte, Count (1800–91), Prussian General, Chief-of-Staff, reorganized Prussian army as military instrument of Bismarck's politics.

Victoria, Queen of England, Empress of India (1819–1901).

Wilhelm I, King of Prussia, Emperor of Germany (1797–1888).

Wilhelm II, Kaiser (1851–1941), married Viktoria, eldest daughter of Victoria, Queen of England.

Important Dates

1815	Congress of Vienna: peace in Europe after the Napoleonic wars. Birth of Otto von Bismarck (April 1st).
1828	Bismarck enrolled at Graue Kloster Gymnasium, Berlin.
1832	Bismarck enrolled at Gottingen University.
1833	Bismarck enrolled at Berlin University.
1834	The German *Zollverein* (customs union).
1835	Bismarck's graduation from Berlin University.
1837	Accession of Queen Victoria in England.
1839	Death of Bismarck's mother.
1841	Bismarck becomes Lieutenant in the Landwehr.
1842	Bismarck visits England, Scotland, France, Switzerland.
1844	Bismarck's courtship of Maria von Thadden.
1845	Death of Bismarck's father.

1847	Bismarck chosen as a Deputy in the Landtag. Marriage of Bismarck to Johanna von Puttkamer.
1851	Bismarck appointed Prussian envoy to Bundestag, Frankfurt. The Great Exhibition, London.
1853–56	The Crimean War.
1858	Madness of King Frederick William IV; regency of Prince William.
1859	Bismarck appointed Ambassador at St. Petersburg, Russia.
1862	Bismarck appointed Ambassador at Paris, France. Bismarck appointed Prussian Minister-President. Bismarck makes his famous "blood and iron" speech to Deputies.
1864	Prussia annexes Schleswig-Holstein.
1866	Austro-Prussian war; Treaty of Prague, humiliation of Austria.
1867	Bismarck appointed Federal Chancellor of the North German Confederation.
1869	Opening of the Suez Canal.
1870	The Ems Telegram. The Franco-Prussian War, defeat of France.
1871	Bismarck proclaims Kaiser Wilhelm I as Emperor of Germany in the Hall of Mirrors, Palace of Versailles, and becomes Imperial Chancellor.
1873	Anti-Catholic Laws. Beginning of the *Kulturkampf*.
1878	The congress of Berlin. Bismarck as the "Honest Broker".
1879	The Treaty of San Stefano. Bismarck's Exemplary Law outlaws the Social Democratic Party.
1881	Bismarck introduces his social welfare legislation.
1882	The Triple Alliance (*Dreikaiserbund*) between Germany, Austria and Russia.
1888	Death of Wilhelm I; accession and death of Frederick III; accession of Wilhelm II.

1890	Bismarck dismissed by Wilhelm II and created Duke of Lauenburg.
1898	Death of Bismarck (July 30th).
1901	Death of Queen Victoria of England.
1914	Outbreak of the First World War.

Picture Credits

The author and publishers wish to thank the following for the copyright illustrations reproduced on the following pages: The Radio Times Hulton Picture Library, *frontispiece*, 18, 55, 58, 59, 60, 67, 72, 77, 78; The Mansell Collection, 8, 11, 22, 25, 33, 34, 38, 50, 55, 75, 83, 90; Mary Evans Picture Library, 12, 17, 28, 41, 42, 45–9, 64, 70, 80. Other illustrations are the property of the Wayland Picture Library. Thanks are also due to Liz Mackintosh for the map on page 56.

Further Reading

Bismarck, the Man and Statesman, A. J. P. Taylor (Hamish Hamilton, 1955).
Bismarck and Modern Germany, W. N. Medlicott (E.U.P., 1970).
Birth of the German Republic, Arthur Rosenberg (O.U.P., 1970).
Bismarck and the German Empire, Eric Eyck (Allen & Unwin, 1968).
Germany in the Age of Bismarck, W. Simon (Allen & Unwin, 1968).
The Holstein Diaries, edited by Norman Rich and H. M. Fisher (C.U.P., 1955–63).
The Age of Revolution, E. J. Hobsbawm (Mentor, 1965).

Index